Key Facts of Decisive Leadership

The Business Essentials Series by Philip J Law

First published by Philip J. Law

Copyright © 2016 by Philip J. Law

Facebook.com/authorphilipjlaw

Amazon.com/author/philipjlaw

ISBN-10: 171984609X

ISBN-13: 978-1719846097

All rights reserved. No part of this publication may be reproduced, distributed, or transmitted in any form or by any means, including photocopying, recording, or other electronic or mechanical methods, without the prior written permission of the publisher, except in the case of brief quotations embodied in critical reviews and certain other noncommercial uses permitted by copyright law.

The material and information contained in this book are for general information purposes only. You should not rely upon the material or information in this book as a basis for making any business, legal or any other decisions. Whilst the author endeavour to keep the information up to date and correct, The author makes no representations or warranties of any kind, express or implied about the completeness, accuracy, reliability, suitability or availability with respect to the book or the information, products, services or related graphics contained in the book for any purpose. Any reliance you place on such material is therefore strictly at your own risk.

Decisive leadership is the ability to lead in a proactive, positive manner; it is the ability to control our staff and professionally reach our set objectives. - Philip J. Law

As decisive leaders, we must be positively creative at all times and remember that our staff sees everything we do. Therefore, it is possible for negativity to become the staffs, just as positivity can become the staffs too. So, ALWAYS BE POSITIVE. – Philip J. Law

Table of Contents

Decisive Leadership Introduction 7
As Decisive Leaders, We Inspire and Motivate Other People To Action 9
Driving For the Results 11
As Decisive Leaders, We Have a Strategic Perspective 13
Compliments, Improvements, Possibly Even Minor Advances 15
As Decisive Leaders, We Are Trustworthy 17
As Decisive Leaders, We Build Relationships 19
Decisive Leaders Do Not Criticize or Complain About People 28
As Decisive Leaders, We Set the Bar High For Our Team and Let the Team Know We Believe In Their Ability to Succeed 30
As Decisive Leaders, We Have Courage 32
As Decisive Leaders, We Promote Collaborative Information Sharing 34
As Decisive Leaders, We Walk Our Talk 36
As Direct Decisive Leaders, We Embrace Change And Progress 38
As Decisive Leaders, We Encourage Our Team to Talk And Be A Good Active Listener 40
Decisive Leadership Helps People Find Inner Strengths 42
As Decisive Leaders, We Deal With Failures Head-On 44
As Decisive Leaders, We Get Social 46
As Decisive Leaders, We Get Positive and Purposeful 48
As Decisive Leaders, We Have Actionable Positive Ideas 50
As Decisive Leaders, We Have Gratitude 52
As Decisive Leaders, We Know Communication Is the Key 54
Conclusion 56

Decisive Leadership
Introduction

AS DECISIVE LEADERS, we are the people that make things within a company transpire. We carry out the set objectives and ensure the goals and corporate targets are met.

Whether we are decisive leaders of a large group, fellow associates, or an individual performance leader, such as a sales manager, human resources director, executive chef, car sales manager, store manager, fast food outlet manager, or a general manager, we set the pace and standards of the job to be done at all times and without exception.

Decisive leadership is to continually push the barriers, to stretch what seems impossible and make it conceivable – but without offending the people around us.

Decisive leadership is to promote and raise the bar and lift teams to achieve greater performance. Decisive leadership builds on what is currently working well.

Decisive leadership is to appreciate people for his or her unique contributions.

Decisive leadership is trusting people so that he or she will surprise us in a positive way. Decisive leadership is acknowledging good things and actions.

Decisive leadership includes leadership basics such as connecting with and caring for people, being authentic and honest, communicating continuously and coaching people as well as stimulating him or her with compliments.

Now let's make ourselves genuine Decisive leaders.

Not only does a leader lead their team, but they also direct them. - Philip J law

Have a proper say in whom we hire to be a member of our team, as we are the leader of the pack and must be happy with our staffing choices; for us and us alone have to motivate and promote positivity within our team to achieve our set objectives. - Philip J. Law

As Decisive Leaders, We Inspire and Motivate Other People To Action

AS DECISIVE LEADERS we do not lead by telling people what he or she have to do. Instead, as direct, decisive leaders, we lead by example and influence people to want to help us. A key part of this is cultivating our own desire to help others. When others realize that we want to help him or her, they, in turn, want to help us. As decisive Leaders we are good at inspiring and motivating others, we have a high level of energy and exuberance. We perk up our team to accomplish difficult goals and increase the level of performance from everyone in the team. Some decisive leaders however, do focus on accomplishing tasks in our job description while forgetting to inspire. This is a mistake. Without inspiration, employees do an inadequate job. However, when inspiration is a focus, decisive leaders unlock a level of additional effort and energy that can make the difference between organizational success and failure. The point is that as a decisive leader we need to find ways to inspire our employees to higher performance.

To increase the general level of readiness to change, decisive leaders establish conditions that encourage people to draw on his or her best talents. Demonstrate how improving his or her abilities and performance can be personally rewarding by positively reinforcing his or her change behaviors with encouragement, positive feedback, and genuine interest.

Ideally, a decisive leader that walks the talk is inspiring people to take action because we know the results are attainable. As a decisive leader who coaches communicates, and celebrates big and small progress, will inspire our teams to action through his or her own behavioral characteristics.

The ability to lead is within us all; it just takes special people to bring it out and lead teams to achieve above and beyond expectations week in and week out, 365 days a year, year in and year out. - Philip J. Law

Driving For the Results

THE DRIVE FOR RESULTS is a critical behavior for success. However, some organizations are all push (drive for results) and no pull (inspiration), which ultimately reduces motivation. Conversely, all pull and no push do not work well either. A healthy balance between the two behaviors is necessary. As decisive leaders, we are effective at driving for results we are skillful at getting people to stay focused and stretch for the highest priority goals. We demonstrate high standards of excellence for the work group. As decisive leaders, we do this well as we are not afraid to ask our employees for a higher level of performance and continually remind them of the team progress relative to the goal. If we are not positive and do not perceive things on a can-do basis, how could we possibly expect others to find us, or your cause attractive? Our attitudes invariably direct our results! Beware of being a silent or hidden spokesman, but make certain that we consistently focus our message on items that are relevant and significant to others. Remember that it is not about merely making alot of noise or even giving the most excellent speech, but rather what we say should have a positive impact, this can only happen if he or she says makes a direct connection with those he or she wants to lead.

As decisive leaders, we are not afraid to take risks. Risk-taking pushes us and our teams into new areas of opportunity. Trying new things, experimenting and getting creative are great ways to build team camaraderie, and possible realize new areas of success.

Results do not fall off trees. No, they do not, it takes us as an excellent decisive leader to conduct lots of staff motivation and our dedication to coach staff into achieving set goals. - Philip J. Law

As Decisive Leaders, We Have a Strategic Perspective

WHILE THE FIRST two behaviors focus on getting activity to occur, the third behavior focuses on the direction of that activity. As decisive leaders, we provide our team with a definite sense of direction and purpose will tend to have more satisfying and committed employees. We paint a clear perspective between the overall picture and the details of day-to-day activities. As successful, decisive leaders, we are continually reinforcing the organizational objectives and the key steps that lead to success. Our employees need to visualize or openly see how his or her hard work makes a difference, and how it helps get the company closer to success. Direct decisive leaders know that our opinion or perspective is not the only one, or even necessarily the right one. Gathering options, ideas and input are essential parts of decisive leadership and decision-making. This way, when the decision leads to success, the team as a whole receives the glory.

1. By understanding that people are different, as decisive leaders, we solidify mutual respect and communication and maintain openness and fairness with every employee.
2. As decisive leaders, we build cohesiveness through cooperative efforts by holding employees and ourselves accountable. We know this is necessary to achieve our set goals and ideals.

3. As effective, decisive leaders we realize that our actions and words must not send mixed messages.
4. As decisive leaders we should stay the course, even under duress or in the midst of adversity. We must remain genuine and use discretion in all judgments we make. As decisive leaders, we reinforce our motivation, inspiration, and expectations to maintain strong decisive leadership

The most significant and most influential decisive leaders of the staff are the ones who primarily believe in themselves and their abilities as a decisive leader to lead people. - Philip J. Law

Compliments, Improvements, Possibly Even Minor Advances

PEOPLE THROUGHOUT THE WORLD greatly desire to be perceived important. Possibly one of the quickest and easiest ways in which you might be able to make a desire become reality is simply to offer an honest and sincere compliment to the person desiring something, as well as appreciate their work performance as often as possible. Doing so is certainly one of the most significant motivational methods, we could possibly ever utilize. Psychologists found out many years ago that when we positively reinforce a most wanted behavior, individuals are considerably more likely to perform repeatedly in that behavior. A lot of people really want to do the right thing, and that means we could get alot more positive results in leading a team should you place emphasis on employing positive reinforcement in preference to negative actions such as threats and fear tactics. Direct decisive leaders commemorate big and minor achievements. Decisive leaders invest some time providing positive feedback and celebrating achieved success. A breakthrough is a breakthrough, regardless of how big or small the step toward the goal is. A lot of people cherish warm fuzzies and positive recognition, most notably when it is usually done in front of his or her fellow workers. More often than not, positive reinforcement produces much better results and motivation when compared with punitive feedback. Always give honest and sincere compliments and appreciation publicly, and correct errors privately. Celebrate our team members achievements publicly; on the other hand always keep constructive feedback or correcting of personnel between the team member and us only, especially if we think our words will make the team member feel uncomfortable. Nevertheless, do not avoid the responsibility to give constructive feedback for fear of disputes. Honest and corrective feedback are an important part of a decisive leader's responsibility.

As Decisive Leaders, We Are Trustworthy

THE TRUST COULD, in fact, be built or destroyed over a period of time, and it can be built in various ways. As Decisive leaders, we may easily engender trust by quickly becoming conscious of the concerns, aspirations, and circumstances of other individuals in our the team. The fact of the matter is usually because we have a tendency to trust our associates much more than our adversaries. Trust can additionally be built with the use of knowledge and working experience. People today only trust us decisive leaders with expertise, knowledge, and self-confidence in our ability to make informed decisions. As decisive leaders we are proactive communicators; for this reason, our team ought to hear updates and announcements from us and not from any other sources, or through the grapevine. Proactive communication can undoubtedly help build trust and openness, as once our team realizes we can freely and quickly share information and facts to help he or she achieve success, he or she will respect us more.

As decisive leaders, we can build trust with people by being consistent. When we are consistent (and predictable), members of our group acquire confidence and trust in us. Accordingly, the trust could, in fact, be built from our dependable honesty and integrity. When, our staff, know that everything we are telling him or her is 100 percent accurate and factual, he or she respects us as his or her decisive leader. Consistency is the key to building trust between our team and us.

Be Innovative, be Creative, be Enthusiastic, be Motivated and we will succeed as a decisive leader; we would have deserved it. - Philip J. Law

As Decisive Leaders, We Build Relationships

AS DECISIVE LEADERS we pay attention to the issues and concerns of individuals in our work group, this generates employees with higher levels of satisfaction and commitment. In many studies conducted, as decisive leaders, we are perceived as being able to balance "getting results" with a concern for other's needs. That does not mean that we are not focused on achieving results. Rather, that we balanced specific needs against organizational deadlines and demonstrated our value towards the individuals.

As decisive leaders, we create strong positive relationships with team members.

As decisive leaders, we can not only be honest and speak what is true, but know how to share the truth with respect and kindness toward others.

As kind, decisive leaders we treat our team members, first as humans and secondly as employees. Instead of seeing our team as wheels to turn in order to get a job done, we see him and her as other human beings with value, worth, and dignity solely because of our humanity. Consequently, we treat our employees with kindness and respect - and that treatment is often reciprocated. Also, as direct, decisive leaders we treat people with respect and importance. When we communicate with people, give him or her our full attention, at that moment, the team member feels the most important person in the world. When people notice our focus, eye contact, respect, and time, we will build a trusting successful relationship and most importantly, a strong, viable team.

1. Staff Retention

a. Arguably the most prominent impacting element on an operation's performance is the recruitment and retention of reliable staff.
b. If our team members are not "staying," it is a clear symptom that we are not paying attention to the crucial steps of creating a successful team.

When staff leaves our operation it is because of any number concerning reasons as outlined in the six following examples listed:

1. He or she does not believe in the product or the viability of our project.
2. He or she does not feel appreciated by our company or us.
3. He or she is not happy with our work environment.
4. He or she does like us as the decisive leader.
5. He or she does not like the pay and performance structure we are offering, or
6. His or her reason for leaving can be as simple as offering better remuneration somewhere else.

When team members leave, and if he or she is still unhappy, he or she will let others know. In every employee marketplace, there is an employee sub-society that is incredibly well networked, and a poor reputation on any of the points mentioned above will keep quality and experienced staff from seeking employment with our company or operation.

A successful, decisive leader is a successful human resource manager! - Philip J. Law

If we consistently refuse to change or correct our attitude and working environment, then we will have failed in our step towards building a happy, high-performance team with low staff turnover. Recognition is staff retention!

2. Team Building

a. A team is an active, constantly changing and a dynamic force in which some people come together to work and achieve set goals, targets, and objectives.
b. Therefore, as a decisive leader, our team members and we discuss objectives, assess ideas, make decisions and work toward our targets together - as one group.
c. Well-managed and lead teams will always out-perform individuals acting alone, especially when the performance requires multiple skills, judgments, and experience.

The same following six fundamental features characterize all successful teams:

1. Strong, effective and decisive leadership.
2. Establishment of detailed objectives.
3. Making good, informed decisions.
4. The ability to respond quickly in a high passed work Environment.
5. The ability for a team to communicating freely, and
6. Development of necessary skills and techniques to fulfill the objectives.

The best way to understand our team as a decisive leader is to look at the internal behavior, as individual persons of our team each have his or her own stories, accomplishments, skills, emotions, commitments, and cultures.

Never, ever forget that **a team is like a chain - a chain is only as strong as its weakest link!**

There are always many evolving psychological influences active in every team. It takes an observing eye to recognize individual and group relationships, and the way people perceive each other. These influences are constantly changing; however, there are certain elements in understanding teams that are consistent:

1. Teams are only created when the performance demanded is challenging.
2. When egos are present, the hunger for performance is the underlying motivator.
3. A disciplined outlook is necessary. Basics include purpose, goals, skills, approach, and accountability for the successful application.
4. Often groups are divided into teams and sub-teams, as the decisive leader we ultimately take the lead in obtaining our team's set goals and objectives.
5. Sub-teams at the top are the most difficult and complex.
6. There is a preference for group accountability over individual accountability.
7. A group of people is not necessarily a team.
8. Companies with strong performance standards seem to spawn more 'real teams.'
9. There is always a kind of unofficial but "natural" hierarchy in a team, and
10. Performance and learning are inseparable in teamwork.

11. As decisive leaders, we can boost the performance of our team best by building strong performance ethics rather than by establishing a **"team promoting"** environment alone.

Biases will exist in our teams

People want to be proud to work for a particular company. People want to proud of our team he or she works in and wants to be proud of the results. To achieve this, we need something to aim for, a purpose, a direction, and a common goal. He or she want to experience a sense of achievement; without it, we will have serious retention problems.

It is our job as a decisive leader to provide purpose and direction not only to ourselves but our subordinates – yes, that is our STAFF! - Philip J. Law

It will take some thought and analysis to come up with this common goal. The first step is to analyze "**where are we right now**" and "**where we want to be.**" Are we the market leader or are we the underdog in our city or region? Is that only for us, or for all competitors?

It does not matter what our situation is; we can always find a purpose. Once we have achieved it, we will need to come up with a new objective. Let's have a closer look at what is needed to create this common focus amongst our team.

Three primary objectives need to be accepted and strived for are as follows:

1. An absolute commitment by us as a decisive leader and our team to be No. 1.
2. Constant recognition and reinforcement of these efforts to be No. 1, and
3. Number 1 in what? That is the beauty of it; it does not matter!

This is for us to decide. Our common goal could be as follows:

    a. To be the number one decisive leader in our company.

b. To be the number one Decisive Leader for the region.
c. To be the number one Decisive Leader of the world (all countries our company operate in).
d. To consistently beat our competitor companies.
e. To beat the operation of a sister establishment also managed by our company.
f. To beat any of our companies operations anywhere in the region, and
g. To have the most individual team members in the regional top 10 achievers.

We need a "**common goal**." It does not matter which one, as long as we pick one.

To create a common adversary is probably more powerful than striving to be **Number 1** in something.

Simply because a direct focus against another entity makes becoming **Number 1** a lot more confrontational and will create a bond within our team to achieve that objective.

This challenge in achieving Number 1 status becomes something to be passionate about and the team will have something to prove - and will set out to do it.

The team has become strongly committed. Although we might never reach **Number 1** in the world, the determination of the team will boost results. Create that bond and we are sure to climb the corporate ladder; yes, higher and higher we will go.

3. **Decisive Leadership Principles:**

Establish ourselves as the decisive leader in the office from day ONE. Give clear instructions, verbally and in writing; of what we expect from our staff. Create *"house rules"* and update them whenever needed, the following eight rules are a necessity:

1. Provide a written job description for our team members.
2. Establish our number two in charge. Whenever we are not in the office, we want to leave control with someone else. The appointment of our number two should be made clear in the morning briefing, and we should leave no doubt as to how far the authority of this person stretches.
3. Tackle any problem or issue head-on. Never let problems or dissatisfaction linger within our team or with an individual. Problems hardly ever go away by themselves and could be a source for the start of vicious gossiping and backstabbing campaigns.
4. If we feel there is an issue between ourselves and an individual, or between staff members themselves, sort it out immediately. Don't take sides until we know all the details.
5. Always apply the same standards to each. Nothing causes more harm than treating one person different from another. The rules are the same for everyone, and the penalty for not playing by the rules should be the same too.
6. Never accept disobedience from our staff; after we have given a team member the first and second warning. No matter how good the team member or supervisor is, if he or she disobeys the rules, his or her employment is terminated. Failure to do this is bound to backfire on us as eventually, we will lose the respect that we need to lead our team, with all its consequences. Also, make sure we know and follow the correct legal termination procedures!
7. Never accept our staff being dishonest with clients. Even small "Lies could cause serious problems." Every time someone tells a lie or gives the wrong information, address it immediately!
8. Never accept our staff to be negative in the workplace, including during break-time.

There is, of course, a difference between a single negative remark and persistent negative behavior. Address this immediately as it can be very contagious and hurt our performance KPI's *(Key Performance Indicator)* is a measurable value that demonstrates how effectively a company is achieving key business objectives.

(Companies use KPIs to evaluate our success in reaching targets)

One final piece of crucial advice: Staff like consistency. Make sure we are punctual for the start of the briefing, the break time and the debriefing at the end of the shift. If we start our briefing at different times due to team members arriving late, it will only lead to confusion and disorder, and that leads to chaos.

If a team member is late, do not let that team member in until we finish our briefing and then penalize him or her by taking half an hour out of his or her wages (if legally able to in the country of operation). If we are punctual and consistent in our actions, the team as a collective will know what to expect.

Building positive staff relationships is like building bridges. Be patient, honest and consistent, and we will gain the ultimate team. - Philip J. Law

Decisive Leaders Do Not Criticize or Complain About People

THE SUREST WAY TO DEMOTIVATE and demoralize people is to constantly criticize an individual team member or complain about an individual team member. If a team member makes a mistake, put it in perspective with the things we constantly do well. Accentuate the positive and utilize mistakes as opportunities for continued improvement.

As decisive leaders, we share the glory, but we also take blame when it all goes wrong. We would think or say to ourselves, "Since the outcome was successful, it was because our team made it happen!" or, **"Since the outcome failed, it was because we did not provide adequate preparation, time, resources, etcetera."**

When we as a decisive leader is willing to fall on the proverbial sword and take accountability for our team's outcomes, it will build loyalty and trust in our team we are leading. Also, when we as a decisive leader give all the credits of a successful outcome to our team, it makes us more respected.

Direct, decisive leadership is also sensitive to people's pride and emotions. The simple fact is that all people are born proud. If we call a team member out on being wrong about something and make him or her look bad in front of other team members, he or she will in-turn fight us to the bitter end. However, if we can offer criticism or show disagreement in a positive manner that allows the misbehaving team member to save face, the team member will then be much more willing to cooperate and work with us. Always attempt to explain in terms of benefits, not just our reasons. We may possess the finest personal reasons for why we believe we are right, but unless we articulate our message in such a way that is beneficial-orientated, and discuss what our idea will do to enhance other's experience, we will not get through. Remember that we are merely saying, rather than articulating our message; unless we give others the reasons why they should care, do more, and become more intricately involved.

If we are a backbiter, then we lose the respect of our peers. Then lose the ability to be a decisive, productive, respected leader, and we will fail badly. - Philip J. Law

As Decisive Leaders, We Set the Bar High For Our Team and Let the Team Know We Believe In Their Ability to Succeed

AS DECISIVE LEADERS, we know that success will not fall into our lap. We are going to have to make our path, set our own goals, develop our own plan, and walk the talk that we teach our teams. Positive working relationships also enhance individuals resiliency. Our ability to adapt and bounce back from different experiences, create stronger self-identity and more accurate self-assessments, greater degrees of creativity, trust, and openness to new ideas, higher levels of commitment to a company, higher levels of energy, learning, cooperation, resource utilization, cost reduction, time savings and human capital development, as well as higher levels of project performance in organizations.

In 1980, the US Olympic Men's Hockey Team was set to play against the Soviet Men's Team in the Winter Olympics. At the time, the Soviet team was the undisputed powerhouse in men's hockey. Nobody expected the US team to have any chance of beating the Soviet Team. The US team was a mix of amateur and collegiate players and the Soviet Team had won the gold medal in six of the seven previous Olympic Games. Before the game, the US team coach, Herb Brooks, read his players a statement he had written out on a piece of paper, telling them that **"You were born to be a**

player. You were meant to be here. This moment is yours." (Coffey, **2005).** The US team went on to beat the Soviet Team and then Finland and secure the Olympic Gold.

Set, a high bar for our people, believe in them (also communicate that to an individual or a team) and be amazed at what individuals or a team can achieve.

Staff achievement comes from deep within, it just takes great decisive leaders with positive can-do attitudes to bring it out of them, and then our team will shine. - Philip J. Law

As Decisive Leaders, We Have Courage

DECISIVE LEADERS with the highest levels of employee satisfaction and commitment are courageous. Therefore we do not shy away from conflicts. We deal with issues head-on, and when we see the first signs of problems within our teams, we address it directly and candidly. Some leaders assume that conflicts will merely fade away and the problems will simply disappear. We only fool ourselves with this rationale. It takes a decisive leader with courage to address issues, resolve conflicts, and insist that we all as a whole team are accountable.

Elicit a response, and address concerns transparently. How we articulate our message often has more of an impact on others than what we actually say! However, be careful to avoid the easy path of empty rhetoric, and say something important in a clear-cut way, and assure that others trust us because of our consistent commitment to absolute integrity.

On the other hand, *if we are wrong, be honest, humble, and courageous enough to admit it.* Sit down for a moment. Are we ready for this? We are not perfect; we are not always right; we can and do make mistakes. One of the greatest personality traits we can develop is that of humility. We all make mistakes, and rather than deny and repeat those mistakes, Decisive people admit our mistakes, and failures and learn from the experience, and never make the same mistake twice. In doing this, the wise decisive leader is able to grow and continually get better. If we are honest and humble enough to own up to our mistake, apologize to those affected, and work to avoid repeating our mistake; we will gain the respect of our team.

It takes a great decisive leader to admit when we are wrong and apologize, and it takes an even greater decisive leader to correct our wrongs and make them right. - Philip J. Law

As Decisive Leaders, We Promote Collaborative Information Sharing

POSSIBLY ONE OF THE MOST common challenges in today's companies is the lack of collaboration between groups within any Company. One team is competing for the resources or recognition against other teams. The information is not shared, customers are not well-served, and work frequently gets stalled. This conflict and lack of synergy frustrate and discourages employees. As decisive leaders, we promote a high level of cooperation between our work group and other groups to create a positive and productive atmosphere in the company. As decisive leaders, we demonstrate that we can achieve objectives that require a high level of inter-group cooperation. Synergy is created and every employee enjoy the work experience.

It might be easy to assume that keeping information to ourselves will give us a competitive edge so that no one person can use that same information to compete against us. The opposite is actually true. When we as decisive leaders and our teams share information freely; it does a couple things. First, the collective knowledge of many is greater than the knowledge of one, so everyone learns more. Second, when we share and collaborate with others, they are likely to share their views or opinions with us. This promotes teamwork, and in return for shared cooperation everyone grows and succeeds.

Close the deal (in terms of asking for a specific action): If we effectively transmit our message, then the end of our process must be to get others more involved in a specific way. As decisive leaders we never squander these opportunities to better (and more effectively) articulate our ideas, and motivate others to action and involvement.

The sharing of vital information between teams promotes trust and the ability to overcome any obstacles and achieve positive results; great decisive leaders encourage this. - Philip J. Law

As Decisive Leaders, We Walk Our Talk

A KEY BEHAVIOR in creating a satisfied and committed workforce is the very basic and fundamental skill of being honest and acting with integrity. As decisive leaders, we need to be role models and set a good example for our work group. Bad leaders create cynicism and lose trust when he or she promises something but never deliver it or say one thing and do another, such as telling employees that the budget is tight and to curb all expenditures, but then proceed to stay in 5-star hotels and eat at expensive restaurants.

As a decisive leader or the management team as a whole need to look at ours or our collective behavior critically and ask the following three questions:

1. "Are we walking our talk?"
2. "Is it do as we say and not as we do?"
3. "What example are we setting?"

Remember, as decisive leaders we hold people accountable. Part of what builds decisive leadership, is trust so this way the team knows we will both share success when it's due, and hold the team accountable when necessary. Consistency is a critical aspect of decisive leadership behavior. As decisive leaders, we speak the truth, and we speak it clearly, even if the truth might upset our employee or cast a bad light on ourselves. The best kinds of decisive leaders are not afraid of the truth, and we seek to reveal it, rather than cover it up. This kind of honesty and directness naturally suggests we as a decisive leader are an expert in clear communication. Similarly, direct decisive leaders are often a active, decisive leader. We do not sit back and wait for an action to occur. We make things happen, and often through being able to be honest about our Company's needs, with our employees. Decisive leadership is all about communication! Open, honest, respectful communication is the cornerstone of effective, decisive leadership.

As Direct Decisive Leaders, We Embrace Change And Progress

HOLDING ON TO THE PAST, protesting and complaining just about progress, or outright fighting against it, will not build the credibility of our team, or help get his or her buy-in.

As decisive leaders we will undoubtedly be at the forefront of the change, making it possible for coaching other individuals on the relatively new facts and information; not to mention promoting the positive aspects of what the change will likely do for our team.

As decisive leaders we always keep in mind where we have started from, always use our previous experiences to structure exactly where we are heading, and also why. We put learning and listening at the very top of the list when it comes to building skills and capabilities. Gaining knowledge from past common mistakes will reduce or eliminate repetition. As decisive leaders, we pay attention to absolutely everyone and almost everything. As decisive leaders, we surely have our ears and focus on each and every person, process, and situation. We pick up ideas, impending concerns, problems, successes and dissatisfaction in our employees. We absorb almost everything and act on the knowledge gained to prevent major problems from manifesting. As decisive leaders, we take hold of all possibilities to make individuals feel successful, competent and comfortable in the workplace. As decisive leaders, we are not reactive, but we are proactive by nature.

Change is easy if we allow it to be easy; do not complicate it - simplify it. - Philip J. Law

As Decisive Leaders, We Encourage Our Team to Talk And Be A Good Active Listener

ONE OF THE REASONS unsuitable individuals in leadership positions fail to achieve is simple; he or she fail to communicate properly. Communication success as a decisive leader can be the process of spending more time listening than speaking, and truly learning what our team wants; our teams priorities, concerns, needs and primary motivations. People want to be heard, really heard, and not patronised. Often, at times, instead of listening to him or her in a conversation, bad leaders block him or her out, often look off or show no interest in what a team member is saying as bad leaders wait for an opportunity to speak again and show he or she is the boss. If this is an area where one struggles, correct it and start listening. The one positive way is to say *"What I understand you're saying is..."* By repeating what we understand he or her to be saying, "We are forced to really listen to what he or she are saying," and as a side benefit, it reinforces to the speaker that we truly are listening to him or her and respect what him or her have to say.

When people talk to us as a decisive leader, stop using the computer, put down our phone, and mute the radio. Give him or her our attention, treat him or her with importance, and listen to the message. The feedback may be something important to incorporate into other information-sharing or decision-making, that we are doing with our team. Everyone's favorite primary subject is about ourselves; it is human nature. Social media at large and the *"selfie"* testify to this fact. Nobody likes to feel ignored and unappreciated, including us. So go ahead and make an effort to be interested in people, and we will win the teams gratitude and cooperation.

To succeed, create staff trust and unity among all members and on all levels; it is a significant part of decisive leadership. - Philip J. Law

Decisive Leadership Helps People Find Inner Strengths

SOMETIMES IT TAKES an objective outsider to see strengths that we cannot see in ourselves, and then push us toward that goal. When we knew that our past decisive leaders were behind us, supporting us, we more often stretched ourselves, knowing we will get positive encouragement and celebration when successful. Additionally, as decisive leaders we will look for a balance of skills for our team. If everyone on the team is exactly like us, then we are going to be missing the competencies that we personally do not have. As decisive leaders look to build well-rounded teams, with lots of different skills and strengths and then we call on those skills when needed.

Remember, if we wish to be a great decisive leader, make it our focus to serve those whom we would lead. There are alot of people that want the power, prestige, and pay that comes along with decisive leadership positions, but few want to do what it takes to actually be a good and effective decisive leader. Decisive leadership is, not about bossing people around; it is about inspiring and guiding people towards a common goal, for everyone's benefit. Build our team up, give him or her credit for his or her work, praise his or her efforts and reward him or her when he or she or a team as a whole succeed. There is a saying that states "Be the change that you want to see." We would adopt that to this discussion by saying, *"Be the decisive leader that we would want to lead us if we were a team member."*

The difference between leaders and decisive leaders is simple: a decisive leader goes above and beyond our call of duty day in and day out to help our staff succeed and become a decisive leader one day, just like us.
- Philip J. Law

As Decisive Leaders, We Deal With Failures Head-On

EQUALLY ESSENTIAL with celebrating achievements is to deal with our team's failures head-on. It goes without saying that this is a difficult task. Every team at some point will suffer failures as well as successes. What often at times separates the highly effective teams from the ineffective ones is **not how our team deal with success but how our team deal with failure.**

If failure is not adequately dealt with, it will become an *"elephant"* on the back of our team and will hold us down; no one will want to talk about it, but everyone will feel the *"cloud"* hanging over the team. It is important that we the decisive leader and our team members sit down and discuss what happened. Simply airing out frustrations can go a long way towards moving forward. Be careful, however, as this should never turn into personal accusations. Ensure that everyone understands that this will be conducted professionally and courteously with a focus on how to correct the wrongs and improve; also, that any exceptions to this rule is not allowed.

It is sometimes helpful to get the team away from the *"team environment"* for a brief period of time. Go offsite. Talk through what happened. What did the team do that was good? What could the team have done better? Keep it positive, but do not be afraid to talk about what should have been done better to achieve the team objectives. After we have gone through this process, work on making appropriate changes. Learn from the mistakes. The next project will not be perfect, but it can always be better. Implement some of the lessons learned.

In short, deal with the failure directly, work towards making changes and then move forward and stop dealing with the failures of the past.

As decisive leaders, failure rests in our hands at the executive level, since we are the decisive leader of our team, our bosses will not fall on a sword for us. - Philip J. Law

As Decisive Leaders, We Get Social

AS HUMANKIND, we need to bond with other people. We have to be social to stay happy and healthy. That means we make time for family, friends, and coworkers; not just focusing on targets and work deadlines. What is our natural tendency? We must focus on getting the job done, so we have to remind ourselves to make time for the people closest to us.

Moreover, general research shows that people need a ratio of:

1. 3:1 of positive to negative interactions to maintain a healthy relationship.
2. 2:1 ratio produces a flat-line relationship, and
3. 1:1 even means we are in danger of breaking up.

In building relationships, make sure we include our boss because it is the most critical relationship outside of our family. It is wise to invest time in our boss and look for similarities because people will like people who are like them. Building a relationship with our team members is crucial as well. They will assess whether we are a threat or an asset to the team. So, get to know them, find similarities and help them out. Building relationships come down to caring for people and giving him or her attention, communicating regularly and asking lots of questions.

Key Facts of Decisive Leadership

Establishing a cooperative spirit is the primary responsibility of decisive leadership. This spirit drives the company and our employees' to higher levels of productivity and accomplishment. For decisive leaders to be positive, we must build a cooperative effort by relying on the following four techniques:

1. As decisive leaders, we understand basic human needs and desires and nudge people in the right direction. We know how motivation works to everyone's benefit.
2. We make emotional connections. As effective decisive leaders, we connect with staff under our direction to build an interdependence that foster more long-term gain than individual efforts would.
3. As decisive leaders we acknowledge the need for followers, and
4. As decisive leaders, we understand our team. We take a time to converse and ask questions that bring information, concerns, ideas and perspectives to the forefront. Then, we act positively upon them.

As Decisive Leaders, We Get Positive and Purposeful

TAKING, A GOOD LOOK at ourselves, personally as well as our team; just how do we regard our work? *Lyubomirsky (2008)* discovered that we have three mindsets with regards to work: people can consider work as a job, a career or a calling.

The job viewpoint:

1. Individuals keep an eye on the clock mainly because our work is just a way to make a living.
2. Individuals who aspire to reach our goals and ascend the ladder have a career viewpoint. Rather than keeping one eye on the clock, we watch the calendar in order to calculate our progress.
3. Individuals who have a calling, desire to make a significant difference. We enjoy what we do and do what we love. We neither keep an eye on the clock or the calendar; however, have a sense of urgency - it is time to make a real difference!

It is no surprise that this third category is prone to positivity. Individuals with a calling are found over almost all positions. Janitors and bus drivers might have a calling while CEOs might experience his or her work as a job to pay their bills.

Getting positive in our activities relates to our physical, mental and emotional state as a decisive leader or colleague. Think of getting enough sleep, watching our diet and exercising.

Make ourselves peaceful with meditation and mindfulness. Watch our self-talk (is it positive?) and make sure to have a preference for doing things rather than buying more stuff.

Taking a decisive leap and direction in our decisive leadership abilities is the difference between managing mundane staff and managing highly motivated staff achieving good positive results. - Philip J. Law

As Decisive Leaders, We Have Actionable Positive Ideas

NOW THAT WE DECISIVELY lead ourselves, we take our energized, positive person to work and practice gratitude, kindness, optimism and love within our team. A well-known advice is to celebrate successes. We can also start meetings with a positive moment, where everyone shares something we like to do or a memorable moment from work the day before Or, ask our team to write down three good things about other team members.

Experience tells us, this will not work with every team in every culture right away, so it may take probing and experimenting to find something that fits us and our team.

Dutch people, for instance, in his or her *"averaged Dutch organizational culture"* will roll his or her eyes at sharing appreciation, and will not see the value and may mock positivity, label it naive, or even *"American."* The Dutch tend to see Americans as overly positive and exaggerating while viewing themselves as realistic, down-to-earth, and clever. Of course, this is a generalization of Dutch culture. Eventually, though, Dutch colleagues are just like all other people. Compliments will do them good as well as keep an optimistic perspective.

To create a positive team culture with this group of Dutch people, we would introduce the performance effect of positivity. Next, we might playfully challenge him or her during the coffee break; to share something he or she like about working here, or about our team members. It would not be mandatory. Just praise the volunteers who share something and next, try to entice the others. This is a example of how having once worked with a skeptical team, and how we could enhance positivity as well, even though it may be uncomfortable in our company or in a national culture.

Positive ideas not only come from us, but also from within our team. - Philip J. Law

As Decisive Leaders, We Have Gratitude

EACH DAY BEFORE SLEEPING, write down three things that worked well that day. This will not take more than a minute and can be really short. However, the practice will help our positivity mindset and will make us feel happier.

At work, we can perform gratitude acts such as sending thank-you notes or emails. We should always promote kindness and random acts of kindness. Kindness works well if we designate one weekday to do three kind things for others. If our day is Wednesday, we prepare the acts on Tuesday night. For instance: we decide to buy the secretary flowers; we send our team member who excelled a thank-you note for his or her excellent support towards achieving the team objectives; and, we help a team member who is struggling to improve his or her skills.

Random acts can work equally well. These could entail bringing someone a coffee or helping one stranger with whatever they need, or simply: being a kind, authentic decisive leader.

Several team members may object to the idea of being kind at work when we asked them. It is not easy to be kind in our company? That may be right. It is not always easy in a corporate environment that does not *"do"* kindness. However, we can uplift the others and choose decisive leadership and kindness anyway. Though that takes courage. We may be labeled as weak, idealistic, or be mocked. How kindness is perceived depends on our team culture and management. Yet, decisive leadership starts with one person displaying *"normal"* human kindness and offering a positive perspective... Are we going to be that uplifting example?

Kindness and gratitude give our staff wing; with wings they soar higher and higher, achieving more and more results for us! - Philip J. Law

As Decisive Leaders, We Know Communication Is the Key

WHEN WE ARE DEVELOPING our decisive leadership skills, to become a successful, decisive leaders, we must learn how to listen.

Team members and managers often tell us what exactly he or she need. Being interested in his or her lives, concerned about his or her issues and providing methods of solving problems are all the signs of an excellent decisive leader. Showing respect for our team's capabilities and trusting our teams judgment goes a long way in earning our teams respect for our decisive leadership. Demonstrate our integrity and lead by example. In other words, practice what we preach. When our team sees us following the same advice that we give them, a team learns to believe in us.

This creates trust and builds a team that is cohesive, working towards the same goal in the same way. One of the most difficult parts of developing decisive leadership skills is learning how to delegate. A leader that does not share tasks and responsibilities are often overloaded. This does not give us the opportunity to mentor our team, and helps increase our productivity or efficiency. As a decisive leader, we share our responsibility, our team members feel more invested in the big picture. This provides motivation and focus, which also enhances performance. Communicating his or her individual roles, as well as that of the team is important in attaining our goals.

Clarifying the objectives, helps team member's understand where he or she fits in. Providing ongoing feedback and praise will encourage our team to be more proactive when solving problems and overcoming obstacles. When a team member exceeds expectations, celebrate with him or her and ensure he or she receive recognition. Decisive leadership skills are very much focused on leading rather than managing. Yes, there is a certain amount of decision-making that must be done by us personally, but team members need to feel valued. Sharing with them, picking up the slack when necessary and asking for our team's feedback will reflect positively on us.

Conclusion

IT CAN NEVER BE OVERSTRESSED that 'Decisive Leadership' is crucial to any organization's overall success. Always remember; never, ever forget; decisive leadership starts with us the decisive leader, not the workers. Manage staff professionally, and do not allow them to manage us. Stay motivated and confident in all decisive leadership decisions, and our staff will follow us to success!

Remember these two key point and use them:

1. A lack of management skills on their side does not constitute a lack of management skills on our side; it never has and never will. Remember to be a decisive leader, and lead our team in an ethical, motivative, enthusiastic and appropriate manner.
2. Decisive leadership is undoubtedly the ultimate key to any business structure achieving set targets and objectives. Moreover, negative leadership on managements behalf creates a dangerous, unworkable culture and welcomes failure, so it is imperative that as decisive leaders we always be confident in our commands and be assertive when needed. Otherwise, we will fail as a decisive leader!

Thanks for reading,

© 2016 WRITTEN BY Philip J. Law

www.ingramcontent.com/pod-product-compliance
Lightning Source LLC
Chambersburg PA
CBHW030510220526
45464CB00006B/2736